SIDE HUSTLE

DISCOVER THE PROVEN WAYS TO DOUBLE YOUR INCOME IN THE NEXT 12 MONTHS WITHOUT SPENDING A LOT OF TIME!

Wayne Sutton

This is dedicated to Keith Schreiter, Tom "Big Al" Schreiter & KAAS Publishing who wrote the original book *How To Get Rich Without Winning the Lottery*.

It has brought me friendships, business partners and yes – wealth.

I hope this book reflects their original work with the emphasis on the changes in the last 20 or so years.

Wayne Sutton
copyright 2019

Disclaimer

This book shares how to generate wealth in a way that everyone can accomplish.

Every person reading this informative book will have a different definition of what it means to be rich. For some, it will be earning $20,000 per month and having no debt. For others, it will be having $2 million in the bank and a house on the beach. And still, some will consider it to be attaining less or a lot more.

What does being rich mean to you? You know exactly what being rich looks like to you and precisely how you will feel when you find it. This book will help you make that internal vision an external reality.

We do not claim to be financial counselors or investment advisors; however, we do have a solid background in creating financial freedom for many people. Therefore, we want to share these effective strategies in this book.

All investments have a degree of risk – some more and some less. The information we offer is to be used as a point of reference to help you make sound decisions.

Ultimately, we hope you enjoy the book, but we also want you to apply the contents to your life and reap the benefits. We are here to help you truly become rich without winning the lottery, waiting for a rich uncle to die or robbing a bank. :-)

Enjoy!

ALL RIGHTS RESERVED. No part of this report may be modified or altered in any form whatsoever, electronic, or mechanical, including photocopying, recording, or by any informational storage or retrieval system without express written, dated and signed permission from the author.

earn money if you choose to buy from that vendor at some point in the near future. I do not choose which products and services to promote based upon which pay me the most, I choose based upon my decision of which I would recommend to a dear friend. You will never pay more for an item by clicking through my affiliate link, and, in fact, may pay less since I negotiate special offers for my readers that are not available elsewhere.

DISCLAIMER AND/OR LEGAL NOTICES: The information presented herein represents the view of the author as of the date of publication. Because of the rate with which conditions change, the author reserves the right to alter and update his opinion based on the new conditions. The report is for informational purposes only. While every attempt has been made to verify the information provided in this report, neither the author nor his affiliates/partners assume any responsibility for errors, inaccuracies or omissions. Any slights of people or organizations are unintentional. If advice concerning legal or related matters is needed, the services of a fully qualified professional should be sought. This report is not intended for use as a source of legal or accounting advice. You should be aware of any laws which govern business transactions or other business practices in your country and state. Any reference to any person or business whether living or dead is purely coincidental.

Copyright © 2019 - Wayne Sutton

Table of Contents

Can You Truly Get Rich, Retire Early, and Finally Enjoy Your Day with Time Freedom? 7

If She Did It … So Can You 10

Tony Grabbed a Mop… and Made Mad Money! 14

One Man's Junk Is Another Man's Treasure!..17

Why Some People Will NEVER Be Rich..21

If You Love to Buy Stuff, You Can Still Get Wealthy!...........................25

How Much Money & What Does Wealth Look Like?...........................29

Your Job Will Not Do It 34

When I Win This Powerball I Will…...39

Gold-Digging or Marry Wealth 40

Hitting the Stocks! 40

Write a Song or a Book 41

Amazon Changes It ALL?...43

The Power of 3...55

You Are Sharing Already… Get RICH Doing It!..................................66

SIDE HUSTLE

Can You Truly Get Rich, Retire Early, and Finally Enjoy Your Day with Time Freedom?

Absolutely!

If you're like us and most people, you dream of gaining control over yourself and your life. Making more money than you spend, quitting that job you hate, and finally buying back your life are your ultimate goals.

You know exactly what you want out of life, and you are absolutely sure how you will feel when you find it – with us. My hope is that this simple book will do for you what it has done for me.

"But Wayne, you don't know my background."

You are right. I don't know it yet, but it doesn't matter!

If you are blue-collar, white-collar or a no collar kind of person, it bears no significance to your wealth potential.

If you drive trucks, mop floors or you are a surgeon, that doesn't matter either. You can truly become wealthy and buy back your life if you apply these simple ideas and strategies.

If you are 18 or 81 years old, it makes no difference because the proven principles we will show you in this book simply work.

What would you do if money were no longer an issue? What would you do if you not only had the money to achieve your dreams but also the time?

What would you buy?
What type of home would you live in?

What car or cars would you purchase?

What vacation have you always dreamed about that would suddenly become real for you?

Think about this for a moment because you already know exactly how you want your life to look and precisely how you will feel when that happens.

This book and the simple strategies we share with you will truly amaze you! So open your mind; grab a highlighter if you have one and an ink pen to take notes. This is going to be exciting!

If She Did It ... So Can You

At 22 years old Jennifer was broke. In fact, she was beyond broke. Every month, she struggled to pay the bills, and she was very deep in debt with student loans from nursing school. However, at age 39, she laid down her blood pressure cuff, as well as her crazy schedule and retired at half the age of most people. She had all the time in the world to spend with her 3 young children.

How did she do that? How did she move from being broke to being rich? Did she win the lottery? Did she inherit a fortune from a dead relative?

No! She didn't. What happened?

Jennifer had a plan. A simple, yet, powerful plan that took her from being a tired, overworked nurse to a retired, wealthy stay-at-home mom a full 26 years before her fellow nurses. Her children will always be thankful.

Jennifer started a side-business, her "side hustle" she called it, and for 17 years, she took her profits and stashed them away.

The profits and the power of compound interest made her very early retirement possible.

Is that the only way to get wealthy? Obviously not, but it is a powerful way to do so.

Now, Jennifer had been told just to save 10% of her income as a nurse in her 401K and within 30 years or so, she could retire. However, there was never enough money left from each paycheck to save that 10% consistently.

Rent, car payments, daycare bills, insurance, and oh, yeah – food to feed a growing family took every penny of her paycheck. And in many cases, she had to use credit cards for those unexpected expenses. Does this sound familiar?

What did Jennifer do with her side-hustle money? First, she tucked a little away each week for taxes (yep, Uncle Sam still wants to get paid) and placed the rest of the money into a mutual fund.

Dollar-by-dollar, week-by-week, her bank account began to grow. Actually, she saved $300 per week and with a 9% return, she turned that side-hustle of $300 week into over $763,000.

She paid off her mortgage, purchased her vehicle with cash, and retired before she turned 40 years old! Isn't that remarkable?

With a 9% return on the remaining $670,000, she acquired a substantial amount of interest. From that interest, she paid herself over $60,000 per year and never touched the $670,000 principal.

Jennifer never has to work again unless she chooses to do so. Yet, with all of her free time, she can now focus on making her little side-hustle another income source if she chooses.

> *"Paying yourself first is a great concept; however, most people can never afford to do this little task without some source of income that is in addition to their typical jobs."*
>
> *- Wayne Sutton*

SIDE HUSTLE

Tony Grabbed a Mop... *and Made Mad Money!*

Tony grew up in the '80s and spent most of his free time listening to ballads his older brother Frankie blared from his "boombox." Deep inside, Tony always wanted to become the next rock star traveling the world of rock and roll!

But he also watched television and could relate to another "Tony" from the once very popular sitcom "Who's the Boss?" starring Tony Danza. In this humorous series, Tony Danza played a housekeeper, cook, and kind of a family therapist.

Influenced by Tony Danza, as our young Tony listened to the screaming hair bands of the '80s and dreamed of becoming a famous rock star, he also thought to himself,

"Hey, I can clean houses too – even as a guy!"

Well, Tony finished college, and he did join a local band as a guitarist. He even played at a few local venues. It was fun, and he had some great times, but he was not going to be the next one hit wonder or rock and roll superstar. So, Tony did what many men were afraid of doing. He started a cleaning company and began to clean people's homes and some local businesses.

In the beginning, like many new startups, business was slow. However, Tony persevered, and it grew steadily. His reputation for great work became known to others. Within a year, he hired someone to help him in the business, and then another person and yes, another person. Today, a number of years after picking up his first mop, Tony has four different teams that clean homes and businesses in three different counties. Tony is now 34 years old and has a very successful business serving others.

Is there a dream you have, a skillset you possess or maybe even a TV sitcom star who has inspired you? :-)

Tony had a dream he pursued. He persevered and established a good reputation. But he also did something that was critical to his success. He found the answer to people's problems. Dirty homes, dirty businesses, and a guy named Tony.

When people have a need, and you provide a solution you can get paid!

Solve problems, and you can make money. This is a simple lesson we should always remember.

SIDE HUSTLE

One Man's Junk Is Another Man's Treasure!

"Tell it and sell it" was a local AM radio station I remember my Dad listening to almost every single day. At the time, there was no internet, so people sold personal items through newspaper advertisements and in our small town, through a local radio station.

Dad would tell me often that one man's junk was another man's treasure. And people would sell almost anything by calling the radio station and sharing what they had, what they wanted to sell it for, and of course, their phone numbers. Cars, lawn mowers, coffee makers, and even pets were sold like crazy every day!

Then came the internet. Craigslist, eBay, and so many other sites popped up. People were buying and selling, not only locally but all over the nation or even the world.

Ralph and Jenny were a married couple who had a knack for seeing the good in what many people saw as "junk." They would spend their Saturday mornings going from yard sale to yard sale buying everything from old toys, furniture, clothes or anything else that someone would sell for a few bucks.

Often, they would wait until the people were just about to pack it all up for the day and then offer ten bucks or so for whatever was left.

One man's junk became Ralph and Jenny's treasure in the world of reselling on eBay, Craigslist, and now, Facebook marketplace. They could easily turn $50 worth of treasured finds into several hundred dollars by reselling online.

The side hustle became very profitable for the couple as each week, they would pick up random items and then resell them online. However, they quickly discovered a knack for certain items that they could make a great profit from and also enjoy the stories behind each of them.

They loved picking up old toys, especially the older toys from the once popular Saturday morning cartoons. Each one brought up a memory. Most came with a story of a child or grandchild who cherished the toy, but now, it sits in a flea market or yard sale costing mere pennies.

Ralph and Jenny became known as the "Toy Traders." They not only sold the toys to those searching for them, but they also sold them the story as well.

What began as a few hundred dollars per month quickly became thousands every month. Hence, Ralph and Jenny had the money they needed to literally pay their mortgage and still fully fund their personal retirement account.

SIDE HUSTLE

One man's junk or one child's toy is another man's treasure!

SIDE HUSTLE

Why Some People Will NEVER Be Rich

"The poor will always be with you." - Jesus

This book is not meant to ridicule anyone who has no desire for riches. But the truth is some people will never acquire true wealth; they will never get rich because they have heard and believed the lies of the masses.

Let's take a look at some of the misconceptions and mindsets that are holding people back from acquiring lots of money.

Open-Minded Susan
"You know that my friend Jennifer started a side-hustle as a photographer and was able to pay off all of her debt. She actually retired to spend time with her family."

Closed-Minded Dan

"There is no way I would want to buy the equipment and try to find the customers. Doesn't everyone just use their phones for cameras now?"

Open-Minded Susan

"You can buy some inexpensive properties, even apartments, and have cash flow coming in almost immediately. Plus, in 15 years or so, you can have them all paid off, sell them, and retire in the Caribbean!"

Closed-Minded Dan

"Oh no, real estate is way too risky. I don't want to deal with the tenants or have to collect rent. That is truly not a great way to build wealth."

Open-Minded Susan

"Have you thought about learning a trade or going back to school and earning a degree that will give you a better opportunity for a higher paying career?"

Closed-Minded Dan

"I am extremely busy already with work, the bowling league, and my Saturday golf game. There is no way I have time to go back to school. Plus, my wife is always on the computer, so online classes are not going to work for me."

Do you know a closed-minded Dan? Have you ever caught yourself repeating some of these statements?

Well, we are taught by some very well-meaning people to be cautious. They actually warn us to stay away from true opportunities.

- Be careful
- Be realistic
- Save for a rainy day
- Be grateful you have a job

Let me state this very clearly and with absolute conviction. You – yes – *you* can become wealthy. Alternatively, you can stay stuck where you are financially for the rest of your life.

As you continue to read, you will discover exactly how real people just like you and me are becoming rich every day. We will tell you the secrets.

This book is not for the closed-minded Dan's of the world. It is for you – someone with a true desire to get wealthy and have the time of your life!

> "If you are going to achieve excellence in big things, you develop the habit in little matters. Excellence is not an exception, it is a prevailing attitude."
>
> - Colin Powell

If You Love to Buy Stuff, You Can Still Get Wealthy!

Most people think you must save to get wealthy. Indeed, it helps, but even if you like to spend money buying stuff, you can still become very wealthy!

I was at a meeting in Orlando, Florida when I met Alison and discovered how she became a very wealthy stay-at-home mom all from her shopping addiction! *(Now, she didn't call it an addiction – just a habit.)* :-)

As a mother who absolutely loved to do crafts with her daughters, Alison shared with me that she was always spending money on "crafty stuff." You know...
Paint.
Lace.
Paint.

Wooden Blocks.

Beads.

and oh, yeah, more paint!

Then, on a dark and stormy night... well, actually, on a Tuesday sunny afternoon, she saw these frightening words: "on back-order."

What? She had to have these little wooden blocks for her daughters to paint! She had paint. She had lace, and she even had the step-by-step directions from Pinterest but no wooden blocks.

Determined, she rummaged through the house and then scurried outside. Her eyes fell upon the glorious pile of wood pieces from another project months before. Yes! She cut. She sanded, and she painted! "Hmmm... I bet I could sell these." That thought became a reality as she took the little painted blocks of wood and sold a few sets on Pinterest to begin with.

Orders flooded in! Alison grabbed her husband and showed him the orders. He saw the cash!

In less than one year, her need to buy a set of wooden blocks became a business selling a variety of blocks and other craft material to women all over the United States.

Alison earned well over a million-dollar in sales and went on to develop an educational course teaching other people how to start their own business as she did! She went on to sell over a million dollars in orders for her course as well.

I remember the first time I witnessed her sell $27,000 worth of online courses during one Thursday night webinar – while on vacation with her family!

Alison discovered a need; she found a solution, and then literally made millions with that solution.

So is there something you love *(and maybe are spending money on)* that you can provide to others as a product or service?

> "Choose a job you love and you will never have to work a day in your life."
>
> *- Unknown*

SIDE HUSTLE

How Much Money & What Does Wealth Look Like?

My eight-year-old daughter will happily do a chore for a crisp $1.00 bill and smile so big, it looks like she is eating a banana sideways!

Meanwhile, my five-year-old daughter not only refuses to do the chores, but she could care less if it was a $100.00 bill I was offering.

Same family. Same living situation. However, there are two very different beliefs or respect for money.

Obviously, we are not children, but we must ask ourselves how many times we make judgments about money based on our internal beliefs. Let me show you what I mean. Imagine you are going to buy a pair of sneakers to jog (or to walk and watch other people jog). You find the perfect pair and as you walk up to the counter to pay, the cashier whispers to you: "Hey, this pair is $100 here, but just 2 blocks down the road they are only $50."

Same shoes. Short two-block walk.
Yep, let's go save $50.

Now, imagine you have spent months upon months looking for your dream home. Finally, you find the beautiful home in the perfect neighborhood, with all new appliances and all the special details you desire in a new home. The price is $495,900, and it evens includes a pool and hot tub!

You load up the U-Haul from your little home, and as you pull into the driveway of your new dream home, the real estate agent runs frantically over to stop you.

"If you can just wait, we found the same home, same lot, everything the same, just two blocks away, and get this… it's $50 cheaper! Yep, it is only $495,850."

Now, it's the same $50 savings. However, you are not excited. You were happy to walk a few blocks to get a $50 discount on the shoes. Yet, when it comes to a half-million dollar investment such as a home, it's only $50. And you do not take the $50 "deal." Why not? It seems insignificant and simply not worth the effort of changing the deal!

Money is funny like that. It holds different meanings for different people. For example – you. Think about it for just a moment one more time. You know exactly what the word "rich" means to you. You also know precisely what being rich looks like to you. Furthermore, you are well aware of exactly how you will feel when you become rich.

You are a special person. The person who gave you this book truly wants you to see and feel the experience of being rich. That person knows this book can help make it your reality!

Tommy needs an extra $700 per month to cover his expenses so he can travel and go fishing each week. So with an additional $700 per month, Tommy is rich.

Candace needs an extra $2,300 to send her children to their local private school. For her, their education is very important. Therefore, the $2,300 tuition being covered each month makes her rich.

Max and Helen need $20,000 per month to travel and do ministry work overseas while taking care of their needs here in the States. That $20,000 per month will make them rich.

Wealth and riches have different numbers attached to them, and each person has unique needs and desires. What does the word "rich" mean to you?

Whatever your answer is, we will show you how to get there. It will be exciting to discover which way works best for you as we show you several ways to build wealth and have a great life doing it.

So, let's talk about the "typical" thought pattern that people have about creating wealth, and why it simply will not work.

> *"When you think about how you will feel as you become truly RICH, allow yourself to enjoy that moment. And then, develop a plan to make that feeling become reality."*
>
> *- Wayne Sutton*

Your Job Will Not Do It

What about a job?
What about a great high-status job?
What about becoming a celebrity?

Maybe you could become a movie or television star! Perhaps when you truly think about wealth, you figure you just need a big paying job. That should do it, right?

One of our personal coaching students was a very well-known actress on a TV show back in the '80s. She has played roles in several very well-known television shows since that time. She was a highly acclaimed actress living in Hollywood and raking in the cash... until.

The money was great, but it was only for a small season of her life. She had outlived her money and was reaching out to us for a solution.

If you are going to get rich with a job, it has to be a very high-paying job that lets you save massive amounts each month for a retirement program.

Finding the high paying job, being disciplined enough to stash away thousands every month, and hoping you keep the job without being replaced for the next 30 or 40 years – well, that's a long shot within itself! Jobs are not the enemy. Yet, a job will never allow you to truly become wealthy. Do you want proof?

Step outside your front door each morning and watch all of your neighbors, their neighbors, and the people living down the street all rushing to work. Ask yourself, how many of these people are truly rich?

They are paying the mortgage and supplying the basic needs in life, but they are not rich. Too often, we sacrifice true wealth because we can only see the occupation.

If you have to get up and go to work every day, then you are simply not wealthy. You are not financially free, and that is a major inconvenience to the life you could live.

A number of years ago, when my second daughter was being born – literally while my wife was screaming in agony during birth – my phone was ringing off the hook! Of course, I held my wife's hand and ignored the phone *(great advice if you are ever in this situation),* but it continued to ring.

Was it an excited family member?

Was it someone ready to celebrate our growing family with us? Nope! It was my boss at my job!

A few minutes later, as I lay my eyes upon my beautiful daughter and my wife was crying in joy, do you know what happened? My phone rang – again.

"Wayne, I hate to bother you, but –"

Are you kidding me? A customer has a question and this moment is when they need to have an answer? Is this the memory I want when I think of the birth of my child?

Let me state plainly that although a job is not the enemy, it is also true that a job does not give you time or financial freedom.

Do you enjoy vacations?

Do you want to travel more?

What if you want to take 4 or 5 vacations per year?

Does your job allow you enough time?

Do they pay you enough to take those vacations?

Plus, no matter how dedicated you are to a job, no matter how hard you work, there is only you and 24 hours in a day!

The obvious question is if a job will not make you wealthy or give you the time to enjoy wealth, what are your options? How will you buy back your life and also pick up some extra cash in the process?

> *"Time is more valuable than money. You can get more money, but you cannot get more time."*
>
> *- Jim Rohn*

When I Win This Powerball I Will...

I am sure we all played this game in our minds at least once.

"The lottery is now over $88 million! If I were to win it the first thing I would do is _____."

You can probably fill in the blank with your own idea.

What would you do if you did win the multi-million dollar lottery? Well, since that is very unlikely, let's take a moment to look at some other shortcuts to wealth.

Inheritance

Inheriting money or valuable objects from someone does work for some people, but it is surely not an ideal way to get rich, and it is not guaranteed to work for anyone.

Therefore, unless you can find a secret way to get adopted by an ultra-rich family and then wait for your rich uncle to kick the bucket, you need another option.

Gold-Digging or Marry Wealth

Are you single or maybe divorced?

Well, you probably could marry into more money in 10 minutes than you could ever earn over a lifetime.

But that's not the point of this book.

Those who have married into the billions are probably not even reading this book, so let's keep looking.

Hitting the Stocks!

The elusive stock market! Buy low and sell high sounds easy enough. However, there are a few problems in that area.

First, to get rich in the stock market, you must have additional money to invest, and you need a lot of that money to make any real returns.

Secondly, do you have the education or a lucky rabbit's foot to accurately pinpoint what stocks to buy and when to sell?

Stocks and Forex are both very difficult and dangerous. When you start exchanging stocks or currency, you can lose your shirt and all of your money – very quickly.

Write a Song or a Book

What about writing a bestselling book that will pay you over and over for years?

Or maybe you could produce a best-selling song that plays over the airwaves and drop cash into your bank every day.

Sounds good, but let's consider a few things.

Well, personally I can't sing. In fact, I can't even clap in tune! So my musical talent will not allow me to get rich in that industry.

Hmmmm... there are between six-hundred thousand to one million manuscripts submitted to publishers each year! The competition is fierce and only a few make it to the top.

For most people, these options are not really options at all. So, what else is there for us? If these "well-known" methods are not going to make us rich, then what shall we do?

> *"If you have residual bills, then shouldn't you also have residual income as well?"*
>
> *- Art Jonak*

SIDE HUSTLE

Amazon Changes It ALL?

I remember the first time I ordered something from this new website everyone was talking about called Amazon. It was a book. I don't remember the exact title, but I do remember waiting for it to show up on my front doorsteps. After that, I ordered other books and even some Christmas gifts.

It was fantastic. I didn't have to leave home. With just the click of a few buttons, I got what I wanted at my front door!

I remember thinking, "If this ever catches on, it will change the way people do business."

It caught on!

But long before Amazon, there was a way to simply change a few buying habits, have more convenience and actually get paid very well for doing it!

Let me tell you about my friend Lisa, and how her love for fitness drove her to find a financial system that let her truly live life and meet her goals.

At 32 years old, Lisa fell absolutely in love with weight-lifting and sculpting her physique into optimal shape. For her, it wasn't a hobby or just a drop by the gym a few days a week. Rather, fitness was her life!

She loved not only optimizing her health but also helping others do the same. There was only one obstacle and no – it was not doughnuts.

The obstacle was her job that dictated where she could live and how much free time she could have. Traveling for the body-building competitions was virtually impossible due to limited vacation days. Ugh!

After being introduced by a friend at her gym to a network marketing company that specialized in nutritional products, she decided to give this program a try.

What she did was, instead of buying her nutritional supplements from the local supplier or even ordering from Amazon, she simply changed her buying habits and purchased her products from her own online catalog. Then she told a few other friends at the gym and her job; they placed a few orders each month from her online account.

The network marketing company began to pay her a bonus check every month for the product orders she simply sent through her account. She received a text message one Monday morning at work and glanced at her phone to see that $74.32 had been deposited into her bank account. Neat! The next month because of sharing with a few friends, her check went to $213, and then $764 for her third month!

In just under two years of sharing this account with a few people, her monthly bonus check was greater than the paycheck she received as an accountant. This allowed her to walk away from her job to pursue her passion as a fitness trainer and coach!

It was somewhat like Amazon, just a whole lot better!

> *"When you truly understand that your dreams and goals may never come alive until you do something different - you will remain silently imprisoned in your own situation."*
>
> *- Rome Batchelor*

How Average People – Just Like Us – Can Create Above Average Income!

I truly believe that we live in a wonderful time in history. The power of technology and innovations has produced many millionaires and people who are living out their dreams!

Only a few become rich through their jobs for all of the reasons we have mentioned. However, a job gives what we refer to as linear income. You work X amount of hours for X amount of money.

You literally trade hours for dollars. When you don't give the hours, you don't have the dollars.

What happens if you get sick, injured, or simply do not want to keep striving and working year after year? You guessed it. You stop working, and they stop paying. Linear income is the lowest level; yet, it is the most well-known of income-producing activity.

The exciting news is there are two other areas of income, and both can produce above-average revenue for you.

Multiplied Income and Passive Income!

That sounds great! But what is multiplied income?

You have probably seen someone using this method.

Multiplied income is one you receive when others are doing the work. Sounds too good to be true? Let me give you an example. A friend of mine owns a local real estate firm, and he has 7 agents working for the brokerage.

So every day, even if Robert never leaves his house, he has those 7 agents out in the community helping people buy and sell houses, land, and commercial buildings. When they help someone with a real estate purchase, the agent gets paid and so does Robert – because he owns the brokerage.

If each agent only helps 2 people per month then Robert is getting paid on all 14 of those transactions although he never even meets these clients.

I have another friend named Sam who is a life insurance agent in Virginia. Sam earns a very handsome paycheck for every policy that he writes and makes a great living as an insurance agent.

Let's examine the purchase of a typical insurance policy. Sam earns about 60% of the first year's monthly premium as his payment for selling the policy. Also, his district manager earns 10% for managing Sam. The regional manager over the area earns another 5% for Sam's work.

The district manager earns 10% of the monthly premiums of the policies the over 125 agents write, and the regional manager earns 5% on over 700 agents in this area!

They have responsibilities as anyone would in such a demanding business. Yet, they are getting paid for the time, energy, and work of others.

Multiplied income works much better than linear income.

Passive Income

Getting paid is nice. Getting paid over and over again is life-changing!

When most people think about retirement, they think of a pension (very few of these still exist) – 401K's or here in the United States maybe Social Security. However, this book is not about waiting until you are 70 years old and unable to truly enjoy life to get money. It is about getting rich and enjoying life now!

We will not place our hope on a pension or 401K, and we don't want to wait on Social Security. In fact, not one single person — not one — has ever become rich from Social Security. So let's focus on real passive income and how you can cash in sooner rather than later!

Passive income is important and really easy to understand. For example, when you use something as simple as toothpaste or even soap over and over, *someone* is getting paid over and over.

Do you think it's better to get paid once or is it better to get paid repeatedly? Nope, that's not a trick question. It's just that most people are not even aware that they can get paid more than once for the work they only performed once.

Sally was a pre-school teacher, and after reading hundreds of books to her class day after day, she began to write her own stories and had her teenage daughter draw the illustrations.

"Sammy the Spider," "The Elephant without Ears," and other stories that Sally imagined became her daily story time with her students.

One day, while reading to her clients, another teacher mentioned to Sally that she should publish her books. Sally thought about it, did her homework, made the right connections, and in a few months of hard work, she had her first book published.

Twelve years later, she still gets a check every 90 days from her publisher and every check is getting bigger and bigger as more people discover her books!

Sounds great, right?

For the last 7 years, Tom has been the proud owner of 42 acres of land. Other than the 2 acres he used for his home, the remaining 40 acres was left to grow weeds and brush. Then one day, an energy-based company named Simply Solar visited Tom and offered to lease his property to use for their solar panels.

Leasing the unused land for the solar panels converted into a handsome check of over $11,000 per month for Tom from Simply Solar.

Passive income is great!

Stop Trading Dollars for Hours!

Remember, the first way to earn income is trading your time for dollars. This is linear income and the way most people think about earning money.

If you work for 40 hours, then you get paid for those 40 hours of work. If you mow your neighbor's lawn, and they pay you $50, that is the payment for the service you offered and another example of linear income.

Do you sell automobiles? When you sell that hot rod convertible to mid-age crisis Johnny, you get paid for selling the car. One sale — one payment.

Linear income is the most common but also the one income that has the largest potential for risk! Why? It relies upon you and your ability to work trading your time for money.

What happens when someone is not able to work because of sickness or an accident?

Lay-offs, unemployment, and businesses close every day. When you place yourself in the realm of linear income only, you are positioning yourself into a place of financial danger.

No work = No money

Of course, we have disability insurance, unemployment insurance, and other areas of protection for many of these unfortunate events. Even so, I have yet to see one person ever become wealthy from disability or unemployment benefits.

It's time to deliver our promise to show you how you can truly get rich without winning the lottery. Let's look closely at what really works.

The Power of 3

How rich do you want to become?
How soon do you want to retire and get away from the rat race?

Would you like to know the secret *(the reason you are reading this book)* and finally find a proven way to make it work in your life?

The secret is the "Power of 3" — utilizing a system that allows you to get paid using all 3 sources of income!

Linear — you produce once, and you get paid once.

Multiplied — you get paid from the efforts of others.

Passive — also called residual income — you get paid over and over and over for the work done once!

When you combine all 3 methods, you will be amazed at how quickly you can become rich!

A Mystery Letter

The blending of two industries has birthed the largest opportunity for people like you and me, and now is the perfect time to get involved.

When I was 19 years old, I received an unusual letter in the mail and will always remember the opening statement, as well as how it pulled me in like a magnet.

> "To say that I am upset would be an understatement."

Now, to show my age, this had been typed out on a typewriter and stuffed into a plain white envelope with my name handwritten on it.

Upset? Who are they upset with and why? I read on.

It was a great hook as the writer of the letter explained how he was upset with the current economy and the devaluation of the dollar bill. He said for just $30 a month, I could earn hundreds of silver and gold coins plus, get paid for telling others. So I joined their company, and over the next few months I shared the concept with others who in turn bought these silver coins. Thus, I earned more silver coins and received a monthly paycheck — for years!

I discovered multi-level marketing, also known as network marketing, and I was beyond excited. Here I am, almost 30 years later writing this book. Beside my desk is a storage cabinet with the same silver coins from that company!

Multi-level marketing has proven itself as a viable and exciting way to build an income. However, just a few decades after the industry was proving itself — something changed.

"You Have Mail"

America Online was the first reality I had of the internet. Literally, every home in America was mailed these shiny CD's you could insert into your computer, wait for a dial tone, a shriek that everyone in that era will remember, and then "tada!" You were on the World Wide Web.

And, like any other way of communicating with people, marketers learned how to reach others and get paid for doing it.

Soon, people were becoming affiliates for products online and getting paid for advertising other people's products through blogs, their websites, and through e-mail.

Billions, yes, billions were paid out in commissions to everyday people for simply sharing products and services. Now, this was usually more linear income where you only got paid once. Nevertheless, people were attracted to the income potential and affiliate marketing became huge really quick!

Then came along a company we have all heard of and most of us have used — Amazon. This massive company pays affiliates to share products. Many people today get paid for sending people to Amazon to purchase certain goods.

Affiliate marketing became very popular because someone could get paid for simply telling another about a product.

No inventory
No employees
No risk

Sounds good? It is! But it's still linear income, and you only get paid when you produce.

Until — and this is my favorite part of this story.

Network Marketing and Affiliate Marketing sitting in a tree... k-i-s-s-i-n-g.

First came love... then came marriage... then birthed forth your key to becoming rich!

Imagine for a moment the simplicity of just telling people about a product or service *(kind of like telling people about Amazon)* and then you get paid each and every time someone orders that product.

It gets so much better!

Now imagine not only getting paid every time you order a product — *literally forever* — but you also get paid when you share the products or services with others...

and when they share...

and when they share...

and when they share...

You can obviously see where we are going with this!

Linear Income — you get paid for telling people about the products or service.

Multiplied Income — you get paid for every one you share with, everyone they share with, and on and on.

Passive Income — you get paid each and every time anyone in this referral network orders a product or uses a service.

This is how you create major wealth!

But, wait...
This almost sounds like one of those "pyramid" things. Actually, it is so far beyond one of those "things" that I want to share the following with you.

The richest man *(at the time I typed out these words)* in the world is Jeff Bezos of Amazon.

Now, Jeff gets paid when someone orders a product from Amazon (linear), when someone tells someone else and that person orders (multiplied), and every single time someone orders again (passive). Do you want to be like Jeff?

When you marry the power of multi-level marketing with the simplicity and power of affiliate marketing, you have the key to unlock wealth unlike ever before in the history of the world!

Beyond Affiliate Marketing!
Beyond Multi-Level Marketing Alone!
And, well beyond working 40+ hours at a job!

If you are finally ready to take control of your money and get rich without winning the lottery or robbing a bank, then let's chat for just a second about the person who gave you this book. Then we will chat about you!

Who Handed You This Book?

The person who handed you this book, like us, helps people set up online wholesale accounts for products and services they already use.

And, then the person who handed you this book gets paid every time someone orders products from these wholesale accounts.

Every time that person uses a product, he or she earns a bonus check — just like an affiliate program.

Then, the company the person represents also pays him or her based on the network of other affiliates and customers in the group — as one shares with another.

What if you could simply hand this book to people, share with them some life-changing products, go online and help them set up their own wholesale account and then you earn lifetime paychecks?!

My friend Patty took advantage of this type of program a few years ago and has retired. She not only trained her family but others how to do the same.

She told a friend how she helps people lose 5-20 pounds of pure fat in 14 days without diet or exercise with a system that she was using. She went online and helped her friend set up an account. Simple.

Her friend Jennifer started using some of the products, and Patty received a nice referral check for telling Jennifer.

Then Jennifer shared the products with her mom, as well as a co-worker. They wanted to get the products, so Jennifer helped them set up a wholesale account also.

Now, Jennifer gets a referral check every week her mom and co-worker Tina orders products.

However, Patty also gets a check for every product that Jennifer, her mom, and her co-worker Tina orders!

Think about this for a moment?

How many times have you told people about products that you have ordered from Amazon or another site on the internet?

Has any company ever sent you a check?

Patty told Jennifer and helped her set up an account. Jennifer told a few people who told a few people who told some people too. Today, Patty and her husband Herb own a home in Fort Mill, SC and a beautiful lakefront home in Lake Norman, NC.

They are literally paid more per week than most people earn per year, and they did it without winning the lottery, waiting for a rich relative to die, and without robbing a bank!

They combined the power of network marketing with the simplicity of affiliate marketing. Just by helping others set up wholesale accounts, they have truly become very rich!

You Are Sharing Already... Get RICH Doing It!

How many times have you recommended a product, restaurant, website or a show to binge watch on Netflix?

When was the last time you received a bonus referral check for your kind words?

When you use a proven system like the person who gave you this book, you'll be able to get paid when you make a recommendation, when that person makes a recommendation, and on and on.

What if you could pay off all of your debt in months instead of years?

What if you could finally take that vacation you have only dreamed about until now?

What if you could, like me, walk into your boss' office and tell him you simply don't have time to keep helping him out — and fire your boss?!

Most importantly, what would you do if you could replace your job and retire early?

What would you do with your time if you didn't have to go to a job ever again?

You know exactly what the word "rich" looks like to you, and you know exactly how you will feel when you find that.

The person who gave you this book is getting paid referral checks from all 3 income streams we talked about earlier. How? He or she is becoming rich, truly financially wealthy, simply by giving this book to people just like you.

Now, this isn't for everyone. It may be for you.

It may not be for you. This book and the person who gave it to you simply give you another option to create wealth.

Can you imagine giving out this book and sharing recommendations with people who are open to a real opportunity? Are you open to discovering more? Are you curious yet?

WANT TO KNOW MORE?

Get back to the person who gave you this book to discover the step-by-step plan to truly retire rich in the next 14 months – or less.

This book was loaned to you or possibly given as a gift by:

```
┌─────────────────────────────────┐
│                                 │
│                                 │
│                                 │
│                                 │
└─────────────────────────────────┘
```

To order additional copies of this book contact the author directly at 910-233-2511 by phone or text, or simply go to

http://bit.ly/order-new-books

www.ingramcontent.com/pod-product-compliance
Lightning Source LLC
Chambersburg PA
CBHW070459220526
45466CB00004B/1883